POEMS
FOR ALL SEASONS

By
Mary Ann Diorio

TopNotch Press
Merchantville, New Jersey

POEMS FOR ALL SEASONS
by MaryAnn Diorio
Published by TopNotch Press
A Division of MaryAnn Diorio Books
PO Box 1185
Merchantville, NJ 08109
Copyright 2020 by MaryAnn Diorio
All rights reserved. This publication—or any part thereof—may not be reproduced, scanned, stored in, or introduced into a retrieval system, or transmitted or distributed, in any printed or electronic form, or by any means (electronic, mechanical, photocopying, recording, or otherwise) without the prior written permission of the copyright owner, author, and publisher of this book, Dr. MaryAnn Diorio. Please do not participate in or encourage piracy of copyrighted materials in violation of the author's rights. Purchase only authorized editions.

Softcover Edition: ISBN: 978-0-930037-98-7
Hardcover Edition: ISBN: 978-0-93007-99-4
Electronic Edition: ISBN: 978-0-930037-97-0

Library of Congress Control Number: 2020920152

NOTE: This book is licensed for your personal enjoyment only. This book may not be re-sold, re-published, or copied. Additional readers should purchase an additional copy out of respect for the author's hard work.

While the author has made every effort to provide accurate Internet addresses at the time of publication, neither the publisher nor the author assumes any responsibility for errors or for changes that occur after publication. Further, the publisher and author do not have any control over and do not assume any responsibility for author or third-party websites or their content.

Book Cover Design: MaryAnn Diorio
CANVA Beautiful Vintage Template

*To my Lord and Savior Jesus Christ
in Whom I live and move and have my being
And to all those whose souls are fed by poetry*

Acknowledgments

This book of poetry reflects years of writing supported by wonderful people. First and foremost, I would like to thank my husband Dominic who has always encouraged me in my writing. He has done so not only through his words, but also through his actions. He has done the grocery shopping, cooking, and cleaning so that I would have time to write. I cannot thank you enough, Honey, for the great blessing you have been to me.

I would also like to thank my precious daughters, Gina and Lia, for their faithful support throughout the years as well. As children, they endured far too many pizza nights so that their mom could write. They have also prayed for me and encouraged me during the difficult times. Thank you, my beautiful girls, for believing in the dream.

Last, but certainly not least, I wish to thank my Lord and Savior Jesus Christ Who gave me the writing gift in the first place. May every word I write, every thought I think, and every breath I take glorify You.

Contents

Acknowledgments 5
Poetic Form: The Diorion 1
Haikus 3
Limericks 7
Invasion 9
All Is Well with HTML 11
Tempest 13
Ever-Presence 15
Aerodynamics 17
Joy-Burst 19
The Minute Woman 21
The Sounding 23
Truth Be Known 25
The Wishing Well 27
The Crossing 29
Cross Pollination 31
Half-Full 33
I Am the Way, the Truth, the Life 35
The Potter and the Clay 37
One Thing I Do 39
Be Still 41
I Walk by Faith 43
The Seamstress 45
Freedom 47

Sock It to Me!	49
The Birth	51
The Beauty of Stars	53
Exhortation	55
It Matters That You Tried	57
Bird Sense	59
Consider Not	61
Revelation	63
Other Tongues	65
Arc of the Covenant	67
Liberation	69
Deception	71
Heartlock	73
Moonsicles	75
Raceless	77
Simplicity	79
Love	81
Trust	83
Carpe Diem	85
Christmas	87
Sunshine	89
I Gaze upon Your Splendid Face	91
Dreamers	93
Daily Treasure	95
Perseverance	97
Bedtime Traveler	99
The Faithful Shepherd	101

Papa Poet 103
Grammatically Speaking 105
The Tree Closet 107
Italian Poems 109
A Te, Carissima Mamma! 111
Giglio di Maggio 113
A Mia Madre 115
ABOUT THE AUTHOR 119
Other Books by MaryAnn Diorio 121
HOW TO LIVE FOREVER 137

Poetic Form: The Diorion

This poem is written in a form I conceived and created called the ***Diorion*** (pronounced "dee-or'-ee-on) in December 2005. The form is named after my husband's surname of Diorio. The ***Diorion*** originated in Millville, New Jersey, and consists of 7 lines of 7 syllables each with a rhyme scheme of *ababccc*.

Majestic Mercy

He sits atop Mount Zion,
All-seeing and all-knowing.
He rules valiant Orion,
And sets the rivers flowing.
His endless love paternal
Removes all sin infernal
And offers life eternal.

Haikus

I.

Monarch butterfly
Flutters gaily to and fro,
Lights on marigold.

II.

Monarch butterfly
Flits across the meadow lush,
Jewel in nature's crown.

III.

Lonely nightingale
Sings nocturnal melody
In a moonlit tree.

IV.

Weeping willow tree,
Branches bearing tired leaves
Bending toward the earth.

V.

Weeping willow tree
Bending heavy branches low.
Old man bent with age.

VI.

Wooden window box
Celebrates geraniums
Bending in the breeze.

VII.

Fragile dandelion,
Kissed by breath of human lips,
Floats in summer wind.

VIII.

Rushing rivulet,
Racing toward its mother lode,
Stretching open arms.

IX.

Pleated marigold
Wears her haberdashery
Like a golden crown.

X.

Cerulean sky
Proclaiming God's creation.
So shall I do, too.

XI.

November's last leaves,
Clinging to my maple tree,
Season's final dance.

XII.

Hurting from a fall,
Stiff muscles scream in protest.
Matter over mind.

XIII.

Sunshine on my day.
In spite of many trials,
I closely cling to God.

Limericks

There once was a writer from Nenn,
Who crafted great prose with her pen,
But one day she chose
To give up her prose
And never was heard from again.

* * *

There once was a writer from Wrenn,
who wielded a fast-moving pen.
When tempted to stop,
she heeded her Pop,
and started all over again.

* * *

This morning I had a great scare.
While hiking, I met with a bear.
His mouth gave a roar,
His paw gave a soar,
Like lightning I flashed out of there.

* * *

I woke up this morning at five,
And thanked God that I was alive.
I got on my knees
And said, "Lord, would You please
provide me with wisdom to thrive."

Invasion

An earthquake occurred Christmas morn
When Jesus our Savior was born.
Invading the earth,
Through virginal birth,
He rescued creation forlorn.

All Is Well with HTML

Designing a web page is fun
When one understands how it's done.
For knowledge supplies
Rebuttal to lies
That programming's something to shun.

Tempest

The raging wind shouts fury
to ancient trees that sway in fierce rebellion,
blindly beating wrinkled arms
against a moving target
that arrogantly dodges every lashing.

Ever-Presence

Tho' I stumble as I go,
Still You lift me with Your hand.
Tho' I weaken 'gainst the foe,
Still You're there to help me stand.

Aerodynamics

The unsuspecting bumblebee
defies aerodynamically
the laws of flight.
He takes to wing without a care
and aviates, quite unaware
he has no might.
There's nothing like the bumblebee
to help the weak in faith to see
the simple law
that when we think we can, we can,
and when we think we can't, we can't—
And that is all.

To My Daughter Lia

Joy-Burst

Today I bought a pretty frame,
for one whose name
brings joy to me
as tenderly
I think of her with great delight.
She is a light
to all she meets,
and nothing beats
the way she bursts into a room
and makes it bloom
with happiness—
and nothing less.

To My Daughter Gina

The Minute Woman

She loves to talk of politics,
election picks
and candidates,
the rights of states,
and founding fathers' policy
to keep men free
and nation strong—
to right the wrong.
Her mission is the truth to speak.
In style unique,
she stands for right
and spreads the light.

The Sounding

I make Your love my greatest aim.
Your holy Name
becomes to me
a symphony
of everlasting resonance,
a permanence
of sound sublime
throughout all time.
And deep into eternity,
Your love for me
remains secure—
a haven sure.

Truth Be Known

The time has come to lay to rest
the lies that test
the truth that frees
and gives the keys
to everlasting liberty.
Serenity
enters the heart
when lies depart.
For truth alone can liberate
and set men straight.
In Christ alone,
the truth is known.

The Wishing Well

I linger at the wishing well,
    to hear it tell
      of destiny
    that calls to me.

An echo rises from the deep
    and makes a steep
      ascent to say,
    "I'm on My way."

I whisper back a dream untold
    and watch unfold
      a mystery—
    God speaks to me.

The Crossing

Blue blood dripped from His forehead
as screaming crowds hurled curses of invective.
Ignominy lay ahead.
Obliged by love's objective,
He razed their hatred with grace-full perspective.

Cross Pollination

Like bee that drinks in nectar,
I penetrate Your Word and drink its essence.
And there I find elixir
That functions as a fixer
Of woundedness healed by Your wondrous Presence.

Half-Full

See the rainbow,
Not the cloud
Hear the silent,
Not the loud.
Touch the pleasure.
Not the pain.
Feel the sunshine,
Not the rain.

I Am the Way, the Truth, the Life

I am the Way, the Truth, the Life,
The First, the Last, and In-Between,
I am the Victor over strife,
The One Who powers every dream.

The One Who launches every star,
I am the Way, the Truth, the Life,
Who chases prodigals afar
And catches them with blessings rife.

I am the Door that opens wide
to burdened hearts beset with sin,
I am the Way, the Truth, the Life,
All who repent may enter in.

I am the Lover, Lord, and King
Preparing for My Bride, My Wife,
A kingdom full of all good things,
I am the Way, the Truth, the Life.

The Potter and the Clay

You are the Potter,
I am the clay.
Yours to command,
Mine to obey.
Yours to design,
Mine to display.
You are the Potter,
I am the clay.

One Thing I Do

One thing I do,
One thing I seek,
Humbly to sit
At my Master's feet.

One path I take,
One road I trod,
The narrow road
That leads to my God.

Be Still

Be still, My child, and know that I am God,
The everlasting Counselor and King.
Receive the comfort of My staff and rod,
And all your cares and burdens to Me bring.
Lift up your eyes unto the hills above
And find the peace and help I long to give.
Be ever mindful of My gracious love,
And know that by My power you shall live.
For in the day you sought Me, I was found,
And in the day you called, I heard your prayer.
And when at night you wept, I heard the sound
And wiped away the tears of your despair.
Be still, My child, and know that I am He
Who holds you in His heart eternally.

I Walk by Faith

I walk by faith,
And not by sight,
Tho' great the storm,
Tho' black the night.
I listen not
To doubt or fear,
But to Your Word,
I turn my ear
And place my trust
In It alone,
And count Your
promises
As done.

The Seamstress

(For my mother-in-law, Natalia Diorio)

>Bony fingers pulling thread,
>In, out, in out.
>Mending memories of the dead,
>In, out, in, out.
>Stitching futures in their stead,
>In, out, in, out.
>Patching generations wed.
>Out, in, out, in.

Freedom

Cast in shadows numbed by night,
He rides the alabaster milky way of thought,
Unshackled by the filament of feeling
That penetrates a lesser soul.

High, high, high he soars,
A pedigree of potency and act,
Fleeing primal screams in hot pursuit
Of neo-natal memories bathed in blood.

Till suddenly, with breathless shock of flight,
He crashes into darknesses of night
That send him reeling, senseless, from his fight,
Into the loving arms of Holy Light.

Sock It to Me!

The Law of Compensation
Says what I sow, I'll reap.
So, naturally, I try to sow with care.
But when it comes to washing socks,
This law just goes awry.
For though I sow in twos,
I reap in spares.

The Birth

I can't hold back the fleeting wings of time
That carry you beyond maternal reach,
Nor close my eyes to nature and to each
New dawning of your destiny sublime.

Nor can I e'er recapture or refine
Those precious moments when I would beseech
The Lord above to guide you and to teach,
For though I wished it so, you were not mine.

Oh, wings of time that lift my love-child high
Above the longing of a mother's breast,
Be patient as I dry a tear and sigh
A prayer of blessings for my baby's best.
Tho' heart would break, I choose to set you free
And loose you to your rightful destiny.

The Beauty of Stars

The bright stars are diamonds
That clutter the sky
Like millions of jewels
Till morning comes nigh.

The stars are like diamonds
That shine upon earth,
Changing feelings of sorrow
To feelings of mirth.

Exhortation

You are a celebration!
A hallelujah chorus in
human score.
Touched by Eternal Love,
You are a hope augmented
to eternal joy.
In you lie possibilities
unsung,
Waiting to resound
Through sweet surrender
to His will.
Conductor He, Who leads
with loving hand
And wants to make of you
a symphony.

It Matters That You Tried

It matters that you tried,
Though victory slipped
through your hand
And left you broken-hearted.

It matters that you tried,
Though setbacks came
across your path
And blocked what you had started.

What matters even more though,
Amid defeat and pain,
Is that you have the courage
To start your race again.

Bird Sense

His jacket flapped against the wind
as he approached the wall
atop which sat a speckled bird
as long as he was tall.
It was no ordinary bird,
but, rather, one quite rare.
He offered him some cockle bread
and cried, "Now I do dare
you fly to that old window there
as fast as fly you may."
The bird let out a whistle long
and flew into the day.

Consider Not

Consider not what might have been,
Consider what will be,
For he whose eyes look on the past
The future ne'er will see.

Consider not what might have been,
Consider what will be,
For he who dwells on things gone by
Will end in misery.

Revelation

The infant smiles while sleeping.
Does he see something
I don't see?

Other Tongues

The rustling redwoods whisper.
Is theirs the language
Of the heart?

Arc of the Covenant

The rainbow speaks of promise.
Does its fulfillment
Rest on faith?

Liberation

The lie begets the bondage.
Why not accept Truth
That sets free?

Deception

Perfectionism ensnares.
Why do we believe
Deeds make worth?

Heartlock

Love is the key to living.
Why do we often
lose the key?

Moonsicles

Icicles
drink moonlight
from ancient
housetop eaves.

Moonlight
throws kisses
at crystals of ice.

Raceless

Why black or white?
Why look at skin?
What will it take
to stop the sin
of stigmatizing God's creation
with unjust discrimination?

Why is it that
we fail to see
the truth that love
is color-free,
that hatred only
blinds the heart
and keeps both black
and white apart?

Why not proclaim
we are the same
in joy and laughter
grief and pain?
Why not look past
the outer skin
To find the spirit
deep within?

O, would that we
would rise above
the pettiness of
gross self-love
and look beyond
the outer man
To sister, brother
deep within.

But only Christ
can bridge the gap
that separates
the white and black.
For He is Love
and Love alone
can make us see
that we are one.

Simplicity

Joy,
Wholeness,
Stemming from
Simplicity,
A flower rare in world of strife and stress,
Emitting fragrant balm the soul to bless.
Philosophy
Of living,
Bringing
Peace.

Love

Love

Unseen

Erupting

Into mercy

Forever reaching out to sinners lost,

Without consideration of the cost.

Always wooing,

Pursuing,

Giving

Grace.

Trust

Trust
Complete
Unending
Surrendering
Abandoning all care to Heaven's throne.
Submitting every doubt to faith alone.
Remembering.
Rejoicing.
Reaching
Peace.

Carpe Diem

Breeze

gently

whispering

through rustling leaves,

Awaken to the life of newborn Spring.

Regale yourself in garments of the King.

It's time to live,

time to give,

freely

seize.

Christmas

Child
born in
stable low,
no place to go,
embracing indignity from the start,
revealing the dignity of His heart.
Come to set free
you and me.
Blood-bought
Love.

Sunshine

Gold
sunrise
bursting through
a purple dawn,
illuminating earth and sea and sky
while promenading arcingly on high.
A blazing disc
warming minds,
bodies,
souls.

I Gaze upon Your Splendid Face

I gaze upon Your splendid face,
Enthralled by Your amazing grace,
As tenderly You cradle hearts
So broken by life's fiery darts.

And as You heal the wounded place
I gaze upon Your splendid face
Till suddenly the joy song starts,
Supreme above all human arts.

Restoring all those hurting hearts.
For as You soften hardened parts,
I gaze upon Your splendid face
And watch with awe as You erase

The hurt and with Your love outsmart
The one who shot the fiery dart
And draw me to Your warm embrace.
I gaze upon Your splendid face.

Dreamers

Dreamers see what is unseen,
Hear what is unheard.
Dreamers listen to a voice
That reason deems absurd.

Daily Treasure

Let each day so treasured be
As tho' it were my last,
And let each moment that I live
Become a fruitful past.

Perseverance

When you reach for a star
Tho' it seems very far
Press on.

Bedtime Traveler

Books are like airplanes
Soaring on high,
Taking me to distant lands,
Far across the sky.

The Faithful Shepherd

When you come to a fork in the road of life,
And you don't know which way to go,
Just remember that God is your faithful guide,
If you listen to Him, you will know.

For Dad

Papa Poet

Memories stir from times gone by
Of Daddy's taking time, like caring nurses.
Next to him, wide-eyed, sat I,
Eager for a laugh or cry,
As Daddy read from *Oxford Book of Verses*.

Grammatically Speaking

Grammar is a treasure,
Especially when you measure
The pros and cons of life without its rule.
A state totalitarian
Would stifle the grammarian,
While free men look on grammar as a tool.

Of course, there are the cynics
Who criticize the gimmicks
Grammarians must use to plead their case.

But whatever your position,
Remember the physician
Of grammar may just help you to save face.

The Tree Closet

(a take-off on Joyce Kilmer's poem titled "Trees")

I think that I shall never see
A closet lovely as a tree
So I will make it my delight
To save my closet from its plight,
By organizing into branches
All my shoes and suits and pantses,
And my scarves, and jewels, and dresses,
And the ribbons for my tresses.

I'll scrub the walls and scrub the floor
And hang a posy on the door.
And then I'll sort and stack and sift
The piles of clothes that do not fit
And gently hang upon the branches
Leaves of clothing and take chances
That the finished room will be
A closet lovely as a tree.

And when my tree is done, perchance,
I'll turn a jig and do a dance!

Italian Poems

A Te, Carissima Mamma!

O cara Mamma, ti voglio tanto bene
Che non ti posso dir che ho nel cuore,
Un sentimento forte di amore
Dal quale ogni mia speranza viene.

O rosa dolce dell'amor materno
Che sai ogni dolor del cuor guarire,
Che meraviglia come puoi capire
Le ansietà del cuore più interno.

Tuo sguardo fa svanire la paura,
Tua voce porta musica al cuor;
Tuo bel sorriso dolce come il fiore
Rallegra i momenti di dolor.

O vita che me desti mia vita,
O gioia che mi dai la vita ancor,
Ti mando tanti baci d'una figlia
Che ha per te un cuore pien d'amor.

Giglio di Maggio

Giglio di maggio, O Mamma sei tu!
Stella di oro, cielo di blù,
Notte serena, casta virtù,
Angela pura, O Mamma sei tu!

Quando ti penso, mi sento nel cuor
Un forte amore, un grande onor
Di esser tua figlia, che sei mio splendor!

Fonte di gioia, O Mamma sei tu!
Luce d'argento si chiara mai fu;
Rosa celeste, beata dassù,
Bianca colomba, O Mamma sei tu!

Quando ti penso, mi sento nel cuor
Un forte amore, un grande onor
Di esser tua figlia, che sei mio splendor.

Vita, speranza, e santo amor,
Dolce conforto di ogni dolor,
Rama d'olivo più bella mai fu,
Gioia infinita, O Mamma sei tu!

A Mia Madre

(All'occasione del suo compleanno)
O donna nobile, di alta virtù,
A cui si volge l'amore e ogni sentimento profondo,
Ricevi questo mio cuore di figlia
Che verso te porge la sua fedeltà.
Tu che sei Madre, colonna pura di fortezza
Ti chiami anche fonte di dolcezza.
A te conviene ogni grand'onor,
A te ti mando tutto mio amor!

If you enjoyed this book, please tell others about it. Also, please consider posting a review on Amazon and Goodreads. Reviews help readers in their purchasing decisions. Thank you!

ABOUT THE AUTHOR

Dr. MaryAnn Diorio is a widely published, award-winning author of fiction, non-fiction, and poetry for both children and adults. Her fiction has won the 2020 Christian Indie Book Awards, the Silver Medal for E-Book Fiction in the 2015 Illumination Book Awards, First Place in the Inspirational Category of the 2011 Space-Coast *Launching a Star Contest*, First Place in the Inspirational Category in the 2011 Colorado RWA *Heart of the Rockies Contest*, Second Place in Historical Fiction in the 2011 Romance Writers' Ink *Where the Magic Begins Contest*, Second Place in the Inspirational Category in the 2009 East Texas RWA *Southern Heat Contest*, and Third Place in Women's Fiction in the American Christian Fiction Writers (ACFW) 2006 Genesis Contest. She was also the Third Place recipient of the 1991 Amy Award for her essay titled "From Feminism to Freedom".

You can learn more about MaryAnn at her website at maryanndiorio.com. MaryAnn has been married for 51 years to her precious husband, Dominic, a retired Emergency Room physician. They are the blessed parents of two amazing daughters, parents-in-law to a very smart son-in-law, and grandparents to six rambunctious grandchildren.

In her spare time, MaryAnn loves to read, paint, and play the piano, mandolin, and cello. She also enjoys sitting with her husband on a special bench by a special pond.

Other Books by MaryAnn Diorio

(All books are available at maryanndiorio.com/booktable and on Amazon.)

Who Is Jesus?

Children ask tough questions. Questions like, "Does Jesus still love me when I'm naughty?" This kind of question can pose a special challenge to parents, grandparents, and caregivers as they teach their children about God.

In this delightful, heart-warming book, award-winning author Dr. MaryAnn Diorio helps answer some of these tough questions. As a mother, grandmother, and teacher, she has firsthand experience with children and has personally faced their difficult questions.

WHO IS JESUS? presents a biblical picture of our Savior in a way that will help your child recognize Him as Love Personified. Little children will come to know Jesus as the essence of all that is good, holy, and true. As you read this book to your children, grandchildren, nieces, nephews, or students, they will learn that Jesus Christ cares about them and loves them with a perfect love.

Toby Too Small

Toby Michaels is small. Too small to be of much good to anyone. But one day, Toby discovers that it's not how big you are on the outside that matters; it's how big you are on the inside.

Candle Love

Four-year-old Keisha has a new baby sister. But Keisha doesn't want a new baby sister. Keisha is afraid that Mama will love Baby Tamara more than Mama loves her. But when Mama shows Keisha three special candles, Keisha learns that there is always enough love for everyone because the more one shares love, the more love grows.

The Dandelion Patch

When Yolanda Riggins discovers that the government plans to build a new highway through her beloved dandelion patch, she rises up in protest and asserts her God-given right to private ownership of property. Will she succeed against all odds to save her dandelion patch? Will tact, truth, and tough love win the day for Yolanda and the children who love her? Read this delightful book to find out.

by MaryAnn Diorio
Illustrations by Valeria Wicker

Poems for Wee Ones

POEMS FOR WEE ONES will delight the young child in your life with its gentle humor, its lilting verses, and its charming illustrations. Studies have shown that reading poetry to children contributes to their healthful emotional development and sharpens their pre-reading skills.

According to Scholastic Parents Magazine, "nursery rhymes, songs, and poetry are key parts of preschool reading. Listening to, and repeating, poetry is a wonderful way for children to learn phonemic awareness." ‎*

POEMS FOR WEE ONES will definitely stimulate your child's mind, bless your child's soul, and warm your child's heart all at the same time. This humorous, charming picture book full of modern-day nursery rhymes makes a great gift for Christmas, birthdays, new baby, christening, and other special occasions. Be sure to recommend this book to your church's children's ministry and church nursery, your child's preschool, your pediatrician's office, or any other place where children's books are read and enjoyed.

Do Angels Ride Ponies?

A handicapped boy discovers the power of faith to achieve the impossible.

Christmas Homecoming – *A Novella*

When Sonia Pettit's teenage daughter goes missing for seven long years, Sonia faces losing her mind, her family, and her faith.

Surrender to Love: *A Novella*

When young widow and life coach, Dr. Teresa Lopez Gonzalez, travels to Puerto Rico to coach the granddaughter of her mother's best friend, Teresa faces her unwillingness to surrender to God's will for her life. In the process, she learns that only by losing her life will she truly find it.

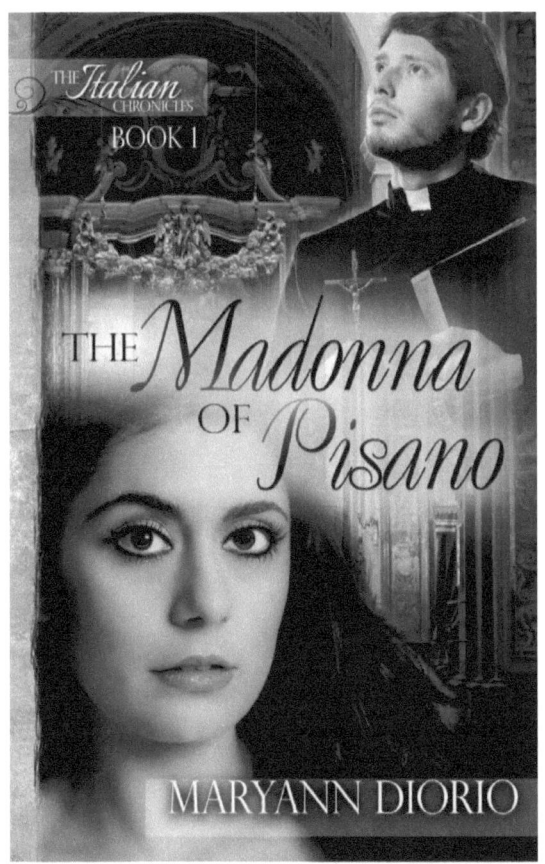

The Madonna of Pisano - *A NOVEL*

Book 1 in The Italian Chronicles *Trilogy*

A young woman, a priest, and a secret that keeps them bitterly bound to each other…

This first novel in the riveting, page-turning series titled The Italian Chronicles *deals with the deepest issues of the human heart. Packed with intense emotion, it is inspiring readers throughout the world with its powerful message that forgiveness can free even the most wounded among us.*

A Sicilian Farewell – *A Novel*

Book 2 in The Italian Chronicles *Trilogy*

A young woman, a new land, and a dream that threatens to destroy her, her marriage, and her family...

A young woman, a new land, and a dream that threatens to destroy her, her marriage, and her family . . .

When Maria Landro Tonetta reluctantly follows her husband Luca to the New World, she encounters obstacles unlike anything she could ever have imagined. Not only does she meet with rejection and isolation, but when Luca is unjustly accused of a crime, her whole world falls apart. Will she be able to trust God to see her through?

Return to Bella Terra – *A Novel*

Book 3 in: The Italian Chronicles *Trilogy*

A mother, her son, and the man who threatens to come between them . . .

When Maria Landro Tonetta receives word that Mama is terminally ill, Maria travels to her Sicilian homeland with her son Nico. She finds herself yearning for the life she once knew as a child on Bella Terra, the family farm, now on the verge of bankruptcy.

Caught between two worlds, Maria dreams of moving back to Sicily with her husband and children to save the farm.

When, however, Nico's biological father unexpectedly appears at Mama's funeral, Maria faces a new enemy to her dream.

But is there an even greater enemy within her own soul?

In Black and White

Winner of First Place in Historical Fiction in the 2020 Christian Indie Awards Contest.

A white woman. A black man. And their forbidden love . . .

Can endurance and faith sustain the love between a white woman and a black man, threatened by rejection, guilt, and racial injustice? Can love alone reconcile their starkly different worlds, lighting the way to a bright future together?

When graduate student, Tori Pendola, a white American woman, and Jebuni Kalitsi, a Ghanaian exchange student and heir to his tribe's chieftaincy, fall deeply in love, they must face not only their own inner demons of rejection and guilt but also the demons of societal hatred bent on destroying their relationship. Will their love survive the cruel and bitter attacks against them? Or will hatred and prejudice gain the upper hand?

In Black and White *is a deeply moving story of the power of God's love to restore all that is broken in our lives.*

You can follow MaryAnn on the social media platforms below:

Website: www.maryanndiorio.com

Amazon Author Central: http://www.amazon.com/author/maryanndiorio

BookBub.com: https://www.bookbub.com/authors/maryann-diorio

Facebook: http://www.Facebook.com/DrMaryAnnDiorio

Twitter: http://Twitter.com/@DrMaryAnnDiorio

Goodreads: http://www.goodreads.com/DrMaryAnn

LinkedIn: https://www.linkedin.comn/in/maryann-diorio-phd-dmin-mfa-99924513

Pinterest:.pinterest.com/drmaryanndiorio/

Instagram: https://www.instagram.comn/drmaryanndiorio/

Library Thing: http://www.librarything.com/profile/drmaryanndiorio

YouTube: http://www.youtube.com/user/drmaryanndiorio/

You can also reach MaryAnn at her email address: maryann@maryanndiorio.com.

HOW TO LIVE FOREVER

Eternal life is a free gift offered by God to anyone who chooses to accept it. All it takes is a sincere sorrow for your sins (contrition) and a quality decision to turn away from your sins (repentance) and begin living for God.

In John 3:3, Jesus said, "Unless a man is born again, he cannot see the Kingdom of God." What does it mean to be "born again?" Simply put, it means to be restored to fellowship with God.

Man is made up of three parts: spirit, soul, and body (I Thessalonians 5:23). Your spirit is who you really are; your soul is comprised of your mind, your will, and your emotions; and your body is the housing for your spirit and your soul. You could call your body your "earth suit."

When we are born into this world, we are born with a spirit that is separated from God. As a result, it is a spirit without life because God alone is the Source of life. You may have heard this condition referred to as "original sin." Why is every human being born with a spirit separated from God? Because of the sin of our first parents, Adam and Eve.

I used to wonder why I had to suffer because of the sin of Adam and Eve. After all, I complained, I wasn't even there when they ate the apple! Yet, as I began to understand spiritual matters, I began to see that I was there just as a man and woman's children, grandchildren, great-grandchildren, and so on, are in the body of the man and woman in seed form before those descendants are actually born. In other words, in my children there is already the seed for their future children. In their future children will be the seed of their future children, and so on.

Now, as a parent, I can pass on to my children only what I am and what I possess. For example, if I speak only Chinese, I can pass on to my children only the Chinese language. I possess no other language to give them out of my own self. The same was true with Adam and Eve. Because they disobeyed God, their fellowship with God was broken. Therefore, their spirits died because they were severed from God. As a result, they could pass on to their children only a dead spirit—a sinful spirit separated from God. And Adam and Eve's children could pass on to their children only a dead, sinful spirit. And so on, all the way down to you and me.

We said earlier that your spirit is the real you—who you really are. So what does it mean when your spirit—the real you—is separated from God? It means that unless you are somehow reconciled to God, you will go to hell after you die. Hell is a real place of real torment resulting from separation from God.

Now God is a holy God and He will not tolerate sin in His Presence. At the same time, He is a loving God. Indeed, He IS Love! And because He loves you so much, He wanted to restore the broken relationship between you and Himself. He wanted to restore you to that glorious position of walking and talking with Him and enjoying the fullness of His blessings.

But there was a problem. Because God is infinite, only an infinite Being could satisfy the price of man's offense against God. At the same time, because man committed the offense, there had to be Someone Who would also be able to represent man in paying this price. In other words, there had to be a Being Who was both God and man in order that the price for sin could be paid.

Since God knew that there was nothing man could do on his own to pay the price for his sin, God took the initiative. In the writings of John the Apostle, we learn that "God so loved the world that He gave His only-begotten Son, that whoever believes in Him shall not perish but have eternal life" (John 3:16).

What glorious GOOD NEWS! God loved you so much that He sent His own and only Son, Jesus Christ, to take the rap for your sins. Imagine that! Would you give your son to go to the electric chair for someone else? Well, that's exactly what God did! The Cross was the electric chair of Christ's day, and God gave His own Son, Jesus Christ, to go to the Cross for you!

In dying on the Cross for you, and in rising from the dead three days later, Jesus paid the price for your sins and repaired the breach between you and God the Father. Jesus restored the broken relationship between man and God. He provided mankind with the gift of eternal life.

So what does all of this mean for you? It means that if you accept Christ's gift of eternal life, you will be "born again." In other words, God will replace your dead spirit with a spirit filled with His life. "Therefore, if anyone is in Christ, he is a new creation. Old things have passed away; behold, all things have become new" (2 Corinthians 5:17).

If I offer you a gift, it is not yours until you choose to take it. The same is true with the gift of eternal life. Until you choose to take it, it is not yours. In order for you to be born again, you must reach out and take the gift of eternal life that Jesus is offering you now. Here is how to receive it:

"Lord Jesus, I come to You now just as I am—broken, bruised, and empty inside. I've made a mess of my life, and I need You to fix it. Please forgive me of all of my sins. I accept You now as my personal Savior and as the Lord of my life. Thank You for dying for me so that I might live. As I give you my life, I trust that You will make of me all that You've created me to be. Amen."

If you prayed this prayer, please write to me to let me know. I will send you some information to help you get started in your Christian walk. Also, I encourage you to do three important things:

1) Get yourself a Bible and begin reading in the Gospel of John.

2) Find yourself a good church that preaches the full Gospel. Ask God to lead you to a church where you will be fed.

3) Set aside a time every day for prayer. Prayer is simply talking to God as you would to your best friend.

I congratulate you on making the life-changing decision to accept Jesus Christ! It is the most important decision of your life. Mark down this date because it is the date of your spiritual birthday. Be assured of my prayers for you as you grow in your Christian walk. God bless you!

www.ingramcontent.com/pod-product-compliance
Lightning Source LLC
Chambersburg PA
CBHW032041290426
44110CB00012B/899